W9-AWT-566

STAR WARS®

EPISODE I

ADVENTURES

GAME BOOK

Jedi Emergency

Ryder Windham

LUCAS BOOKS

SCHOLASTIC INC.

New York Toronto London Auckland Sydney
Mexico City New Delhi Hong Kong

ISBN 0-439-12987-7

12 11 10 9 8 7 6 5 4 3 2 1   9/9 0 1 2 3 4/0

Printed in the U.S.A.
First Scholastic printing, December 1999

YOUR ADVENTURE BEGINS!

You are a Jedi or an ally to the Jedi. The Adventure Guide contains the rules of JEDI ADVENTURES. You must follow these rules at all times.

The Bartokk assassins are using remote-controlled X10-D draft droids to infiltrate the Corulag Academy Science Service tower. You are in the lobby outside the nursery on Level 7 in the tower. An Academy security droid was attacked and bypassed by two X10-Ds who escaped into a lift tube. According to the damaged security droid, one of the X10-Ds contains a concealed plasma bomb.

While the Model E droids try to comfort the frightened children, two X10-Ds have entered the lobby from a stairwell. You don't know why the Bartokks want to assault Corulag Academy, but you now know they are using at least four X10-Ds to carry out their diabolical plan. You are greatly concerned for the safety of the children on Level 7, as well as for Teela Panjarra, the six-month-old Force-sensitive child being held by scientists somewhere within the Science Service tower.

You must stop the attack on the Academy, and also rescue Teela Panjarra. You cannot allow the Bartokks to detonate a plasma bomb.

To foil the Bartokks' plan, you will have to defeat the remote-control droids as well as the Bartokks themselves. If you can learn exactly how many Bartokks and X10-Ds are involved in the murderous scheme, you'll have a better chance of tracking the villains during your adventure.

Choose your character. Every character has unique talents, which are listed on each character card. You can use Power three times on this adventure.

You start this adventure with your Adventure Point (AP) total from your previous adventure, or 1000 AP if this is your first adventure.

May the Force be with you.

YOUR ADVENTURE:
JEDI EMERGENCY

The two X10-Ds advance toward the central indoor playground. Their infrared photoreceptors glow with menace in the gloomy lobby.

"Those droids aren't authorized to be on this level!" says the damaged security droid, unable to move.

The Bartokks might be using optical gear to allow themselves to see whatever is within visual range of the remote-controlled X10-Ds' photoreceptors. You cannot allow the X10-Ds to harm anyone in the nursery, but you don't want to alert the Bartokks of your presence within the Science Service tower. Instead of openly attacking the X10-Ds, it would be smart to make the Bartokks think the X10-Ds had an accident.

To defeat the remote-controlled droids, choose to combat them with Power, trip them, or use your lightsaber against them.

To combat the X10-Ds (using Power): Choose your Redirect Power or your Force Movement Power. You can only use Force Movement if you are a Jedi. Roll the 20-dice to make the X10-Ds slam into the playground wall. Your roll# + your Power# + Your Power's mid-resist# is your adventure#.

If your adventure# is equal to or more than 14, add the difference to your AP total. Both X10-Ds are lifted off their feet as they hurtle headfirst through the air and smash against the playground wall. The droids are disabled, and you may proceed.

If your adventure# is less than 14, subtract the difference from your AP total. The X10-Ds are dangerously near some children. Proceed to trip them or use your lightsaber (below).

*NOTE: This counts as one of three Power uses you are allowed on this adventure.

To trip the X10-Ds: Roll the 10-dice to stick your leg out and trip one of the X10-Ds and make it fall into its partner. If strategy is one of your talents, your roll# + your strength# + your stealth# is your adventure#. If strategy is not one of your talents, your roll# + your strength# + 1 is your adventure#.

If your adventure# is equal to or more than 7, add the difference to your AP total. The droid trips over your extended leg and falls into its partner. Both X10-Ds crash face first onto the floor, then roll onto their backs. Smoke rises from their heads, and you see that their photoreceptors and operating signal receivers are ruined. You may proceed.

If your adventure# is less than 7, subtract the difference from your AP total. The remote-controlled X10-D almost crushes your leg. Proceed to use your lightsaber (below).

To use your lightsaber against the X10-Ds: Choose your lightsaber. Roll the 20-dice to attack both X10-Ds at the same time. If defense is one of your talents, your roll# + your weaponry# + your weapon's close-range# + 1 is your adventure#. If defense is not one of your talents, your roll# + your weaponry# + your weapon's close-range# is your adventure#.

If your adventure# is equal to or more than 13, add the difference to your AP total. You swiftly defeat both X10-Ds. Their bodies crash to the playground floor, and you may proceed.

If your adventure# is less than 13, subtract 8 AP from your AP total. You defeat the nearest X10-D but miss its partner. You must strike down the other droid before the Bartokks realize their remote-controlled X10-Ds are under attack. Roll the 20-dice again for your new roll#. If defense is one of your talents, your new roll# + your weaponry# + your weapon's close-range# + 2 is your new adventure#. If defense is not one of your talents, your new roll# + your weaponry# + your weapon's close-range# + 1 is your new adventure#.

If your new adventure# is equal to or more than 13, add the difference to your AP total. You strike down the second droid and it collapses to the playground floor. You may proceed.

If your new adventure# is less than 13, subtract the difference from your AP total. You miss the droid and almost step into range of its infrared photoreceptors. Go back to "Roll the 20-dice again for your new roll#" and repeat. When you have defeated the X10-D, you may proceed.

As the X10-D draft droids crash to the playground floor, their heads roll away. You step cautiously between the two fallen X10-Ds to reach their armored chest panels. Taking great care, you slide both panels back.

The X10-D on your left contains a plasma bomb.

One of your allies notes, "The Bartokks always have a backup plan, so it makes sense that they'd have more than one bomb. They won't dare to trigger the bombs until they're safely away from the city. But now that these two X10-Ds are down, the Bartokks who were controlling them might come looking for them here."

"All children and adults must be removed from the building at once," states one of the Jedi.

You tell your allies you will deactivate the bomb and find Teela Panjarra. In the meantime, they must lead everyone to safety.

Your allies and the Model E units quickly round up the children and escort them to the emergency stairwell, leaving you to examine the plasma bomb. Shaped like a geodesic sphere, the compact bomb is magnetically clamped within the X10-D's chest cavity. A primitive transmitter is affixed to the trigger mechanism. You glance around the indoor playground and notice a child's sculpture resting on a nearby table.

To prevent the radio-operated trigger from activating the bomb, choose to jam the bomb's trigger mechanism or remove the bomb's transmission receiver.

To jam the bomb's trigger mechanism: Roll the 10-dice to pry a piece from the child's sculpture and jam the plasma bomb's trigger. Your roll# + your skill# is your adventure#.

If your adventure# is equal to or more than 6, add the difference + 5 to your AP total. The piece sticks in place and the trigger cannot work. You may proceed.

If your adventure# is less than 6, subtract the difference from your AP total. The sculpture is unbreakable. Proceed to remove the bomb's transmission receiver (below).

To remove the bomb's transmission receiver: Roll the 10-dice to carefully detach the receiver from the bomb. Your roll# + your knowledge # + your skill# is your adventure#.

If your adventure# is equal to or more than 8, add the difference + 5 to your AP total. You successfully pull the transmission receiver away from the bomb. Although the plasma bomb is still intact, the Bartokks will no longer be able to detonate it by remote control. You may proceed.

If your adventure# is less than 8, subtract the difference from your AP total. You have accidentally activated the bomb's automatic timer. Unless you switch off the timer, the bomb will explode in ten seconds. Roll the 10-dice again for your new roll#. Your new roll# + your knowledge# + your skill# + 1 is your new adventure#.

> *If your adventure# is equal to or more than 8*, add the difference to your AP total. With the flick of a switch, you turn off the plasma bomb's timer. You may proceed.

> *If your adventure# is less than 8*, subtract the difference from your AP total. You pressed the wrong switch, and the timer is still active! Go back to "Roll the 10-dice again for your new roll#" and repeat. When you have switched off the plasma bomb's timer, you may proceed.

You remove the plasma bomb from the droid's torso. Even though the bomb is deactivated, you must destroy it. If the Bartokks recover the bomb, they might attempt to reset it.

"Good work," praises the damaged Academy security droid, still propped up against the checkpoint kiosk. "Sorry I wasn't any help."

"Here," you say to the droid as you hand him the plasma bomb. "Disassemble this."

As the security droid takes the bomb, you hear a hissing sound from the doorway to the emergency stairwell. You turn just in time to see the shadowy forms of two Bartokk assassins slip out of the doorway. The Bartokks drop their X10-D remote-control devices and leap at you from across the lobby. Both Bartokks wield deadly vibro-axes.

Although you are not violent by nature, you realize there isn't any use in negotiating with the Bartokks. They are cold-blooded killers who will stop at nothing to destroy anyone they perceive as an enemy. Furthermore, they see the plasma bomb in the security droid's hands. You can't allow the Bartokks to get their claws on the bomb.

Choose to combat the Bartokks using Power, your weapon, or your bare hands.

To combat the Bartokks (using Power)*:
You must be a Jedi to do this. Choose your Force Movement Power. Roll the 20-dice to lift the two assassins as high as you can. Your roll# + your Power# +your Power's mid-resist# is your adventure#.

If your adventure# is equal to or more than 15, add the difference + 8 to your AP total. The two Bartokks are launched straight up and smash their insectoid skulls against the high ceiling. Stunned, they fall to the floor, landing on top of their own vibro-axes. Both assassins are eliminated, and you may proceed.

If your adventure# is less than 15, subtract the difference from your AP total. The hive-minded Bartokks resist your Power and prepare to strike. Proceed to combat the Bartokks using your weapon (next page).

*NOTE: This counts as one of three Power uses you are allowed on this adventure.

To combat the Bartokks using your weapon: Choose your weapon. Roll the 20-dice to target the two Bartokks. Your roll# + your weaponry# + your weapon's close-range# is your adventure#.

If your adventure# is equal to or more than 14, add the difference + 7 to your AP total. In a fierce confrontation, you bring down both Bartokks. Their shattered bodies collapse upon the lobby floor, and you may proceed.

If your adventure# is less than 14, subtract the difference from your AP total. Your weapon isn't fully energized! Proceed to combat the Bartokks using your bare hands (below).

To combat the Bartokks using your bare hands: Roll the 20-dice to flip one of the Bartokks onto the nursery's serving carousel. If strategy is one of your talents, your roll# + your strength# + 1 is your adventure#. If strategy is not one of your talents, your roll# + your strength# is your adventure#.

If your adventure# is equal to or more than 12, add the difference + 7 to your AP total. You grab hold of the nearest Bartokk's lower left wrist and twist hard, flipping the Bartokk over your shoulder. The startled assassin lands on the serving carousel, causing it to spin on its axis. The Bartokk is whipped around and launched from the carousel, only to smash into his partner. Unable to deactivate their vibro-axes in time, the two Bartokks destroy each other. You may proceed.

If your adventure# is less than 12, subtract 6 AP from your AP total. The nearest Bartokk evades your grip, but you should be able to flip his partner onto the serving carousel. Roll the 20-dice again for your new roll#. Your strength# + 2 is your new adventure#.

If your new adventure# is equal to or more than 11, add the difference to your AP total. The thrown Bartokk is whipped back by the carousel and crashes into his partner. The two Bartokks accidentally destroy each other with their weapons, and you may proceed.

If your new adventure# is less than 11, subtract the difference from your AP total. You are unable to defeat the two Bartokks in bare-handed combat. Fortunately, your weapon is now fully energized. Combat the Bartokks with your weapon (previous page).

The Bartokks lie motionless on the floor near the fallen X10-D. You realize there might be more Bartokks or X10-Ds in the emergency stairwell, so you remove your comlink from your belt and contact your allies. You tell them you were attacked from the emergency stairwell, and that they should watch for more assassins.

"Thanks for the warning," replies one of your allies. "The children and Academy cadets are out of the tower, but we haven't seen Chief Scientist Frexton or any sign of Teela Panjarra. It's possible they're both still inside the —"

A loud burst of static comes from your comlink. Something is interfering with your signal. In all likelihood, the Bartokks are jamming transmissions from the tower.

You are on your own.

"What's happening?" asks the damaged security droid.

You tell him that the Bartokks are interfering with the communications frequencies. After all, the Bartokks don't need comlinks. They communicate telepathically. You point to the fallen assassins and add that if these two warned the hive about what happened here other Bartokks may already be on their way.

"I'm afraid I'm not in much condition to defend Level seven anymore," admits the security droid, looking at his useless legs. He sets to the task of taking apart the plasma bomb.

According to Chief Scientist Frexton, the Force-sensitive six-month-old child named Teela Panjarra is in a private nursery within the Science Service tower. There are still two X10-D draft droids in the tower, one of which is carrying a plasma bomb.

You cannot leave the tower until you rescue Teela Panjarra. The Science Service security computer should be able to pinpoint her location.

While the damaged security droid disassembles the first bomb, you study the checkpoint's deactivated computer console. You suspect either the X10-Ds or the Bartokks are responsible for severing a power terminal that caused both the lobby to black out and the computer to shut down. In the darkness, it is difficult to see the console.

You must locate Teela Panjarra. It's possible the damaged security droid also possesses this vital information. Choose to ask the Academy security droid for Teela Panjarra's location, ask the droid to repair the security computer, or fix the security computer yourself.

To ask the Academy security droid for Teela Panjarra's location: Roll the 10-dice to address the security droid. Your roll# + your charm# is your adventure#.

If your adventure# is equal to or more than 7, add the difference + 10 to your AP total. The security droid informs you the Force-sensitive infant is being held in a research laboratory on Level 58 of the Science Service tower. You may proceed.

If your adventure# is less than 7, subtract the difference from your AP total. The security droid does not know the location of Teela Panjarra. Proceed to ask the Academy security droid to repair the security computer or fix it yourself (below).

To ask the Academy security droid to repair the security computer: Roll the 10-dice to make your request. Your roll# + your charm# + 1 is your adventure#.

If your adventure# is equal to or more than 8, add the difference + 8 to your AP total. The security droid quickly repairs the security computer, which reveals Teela Panjarra's location. She is being held in a research laboratory on Level 58 of the Science Service tower. You may proceed.

If your adventure# is less than 8, subtract the difference from your AP total. The security droid does not know how to fix the computer. Proceed to fix it yourself (below).

To fix the security computer yourself: Roll the 20-dice to repair the computer and locate Teela Panjarra. If repair is one of your talents, your roll# + your knowledge# + your skill# + 2 is your adventure#. If repair is not one of your talents, your roll# + your knowledge# + your skill# is your adventure#.

If your adventure# is equal to or more than 13, add the difference + 9 to your AP total. The security computer comes online and reveals Teela Panjarra is being held in a research laboratory on Level 58 of the Science Service tower. You may proceed.

If your adventure# is less than 13, subtract 7 AP from your AP total. The computer has a built-in antisabotage device, and it shocks you mildly when you touch it. You'll have to make another attempt at activating the computer.

Roll the 20-dice again for your new roll#. Your new roll# + your knowledge# + your skill# + 1 is your new adventure#.

If your new adventure# is equal to or more than 14, add the difference to your AP total. The computer comes online, and divulges Teela Panjarra's location. She is in a research lab on Level 58 of the Science Service tower. You may proceed.

If your new adventure# is less than 14, subtract the difference from your AP total. You receive a stronger shock from the computer. Go back to "Roll the 20-dice again for your new roll#" and repeat. When you have activated the computer and learned the location of Teela Panjarra, you may proceed.

You are surprised by Teela Panjarra's location. Chief Scientist Frexton had said the girl was being kept in a private nursery, not in a research lab. Obviously, Frexton is not a man to be trusted.

You want to go to Level 58 immediately. You check the lift tube near the security checkpoint, and find the sliding lift doors are still tightly sealed. The lift tube controls are virtually fried and require extensive repairs.

To open the lift tube doors, choose to use your strength or your weapon.

To use your strength: Roll the 10-dice to brace your hands against the lift tube doors and push. Your roll# + your strength# is your adventure#.

If your adventure# is equal to or more than 7, add the difference + 5 to your AP total. The doors slide back into the wall and expose the lift tube shaft. You may proceed.

If your adventure# is less than 7, subtract 4 AP from your AP total. The doors remain scaled. You must use more strength. Roll the 10-dice again for your new roll#. Your new roll# + your strength# + 2 is your new adventure#.

If your new adventure# is equal to or more than 8, add the difference to your AP total. Straining with all your might, you push the doors open and gaze into the lift tube shaft. You may proceed.

If your new adventure# is less than 8, subtract the difference from your AP total. It will take more than physical strength to open the sealed lift tube doors. Proceed to use your weapon (below).

To use your weapon: Choose your weapon. Roll the 10-dice to target the door. Your roll# + your weaponry# + your weapon's close-range# is your adventure#.

If your adventure# is equal to or more than 9, add the difference + 5 to your AP total. Your weapon creates a wide hole in the lift tube doors. You may proceed.

If your adventure# is less than 9, subtract 5 AP from your AP total. You were standing too far away from the lift tube doors for your weapon to be effective. You must step closer to the doors. Roll the 10-dice again for your new roll#. Your new roll# + your weaponry# + your weapon's close-range# is your new adventure#.

If your new adventure# is equal to or more than 10, add the difference to your AP total. With deft use of your weaponry, you create a wide circular hole through the doors. You may proceed.

If your adventure# is less than 10, subtract the difference from your AP total. Your weapon almost slips from your grasp. Go back to "Roll the 10-dice again for your new roll#" and repeat. When you have created a hole through the lift tube doors, you may proceed.

You stare into the lift tube shaft. The lift itself is gone, having ferried the first two X10-Ds to another level within the Science Service tower. You don't know whether the two X10-Ds went up or down, but you know that Teela Panjarra should be on Level 58.

Above the security kiosk, an air vent rattles on the ceiling. Suddenly, the heavy vent cover swings out on its hinges and two Bartokks drop from the open vent. As you suspected, they have been alerted by their fallen comrades.

Both Bartokks carry cryogen whips, capable of causing near-explosive chemical reactions when the super-cold lash tips strike an object. The Bartokks land next to the damaged security droid. Before the droid can move, the Bartokks bring their cryogen whips down on him. With a stunning blast and a loud crack, the whips strike, and the helpless droid is instantly reduced to frozen metal.

It is fortunate that the brave security droid had already disassembled the plasma bomb.

You are standing near the open lift tube shaft when the Bartokks turn away from the droid and leap at you. Choose to jump aside or combat the Bartokks. If you choose combat, choose to combat both Bartokks at once or one at a time.

To jump aside: Roll the 10-dice to jump away from the open lift tube. If either strategy or decision is one of your talents, your roll# + your stealth# + 2 is your adventure#. If neither strategy nor decision is one of your talents, your roll# + your stealth# is your adventure#.

If your adventure# is equal to or more than 7, add the difference + 10 to your AP total. The two Bartokks sail past you and tumble through the open lift tube doorway. Not even the body-armored Bartokks can survive the plummet to the tower's sub-basement levels. You may proceed.

If your adventure# is less than 7, subtract the difference from your AP total. The Bartokks stop short of the open lift tube shaft and prepare to strike you with their cryogen whips. Proceed to combat both Bartokks at once (next page).

To combat both Bartokks at once:
Choose your weapon. Roll the 20-dice to target
the hinges of the heavy vent cover that dangles
from the ceiling. If targeting is one of your talents, your roll# + your weaponry# + your
weapon's far-range# + 1 is your adventure#. If
targeting is not one of your talents, your roll# +
your weaponry# + your weapon's far-range# is
your adventure#.

*If your adventure# is equal to or more than
14*, add the difference + 10 to your AP total.
You sever the hinges and the heavy vent cover
falls from the ceiling, crushing the two Bartokks below. You may proceed.

If your adventure# is less than 14, subtract the
difference from your AP total. You miss the
vent cover's hinges. Proceed to combat one
Bartokk at a time (below).

To combat one Bartokk at a time: Choose
your weapon. Roll the 20-dice to attack the
nearest Bartokk. If defense is one of your talents,
your roll# + your weaponry# + your weapon's
mid-range# + 2 is your adventure#. If defense is
not one of your talents, your roll# + your
weaponry# + your weapon's mid-range# is your
adventure#.

*If your adventure# is equal to or more than
16*, add the difference + 6 to your AP total.

The nearest Bartokk is felled by your weapon. To combat the second Bartokk, go back to "Roll the 20-dice to attack" and repeat. When both Bartokks are defeated, you may proceed.

If your adventure# is less than 16, subtract 8 AP from your AP total. You are nearly struck by a cryogen whip. To avoid being hit by the whip, you decide to move in close to your opponent. Roll the 20-dice again for your new roll#. If defense is one of your talents, your new roll# + your weaponry# + your weapon's close-range# + 2 is your new adventure#. If defense is not one of your talents, your new roll# + your weaponry# + your weapon's close-range# is your new adventure#.

> *If your new adventure# is equal to or more than 16,* add the difference + 2 to your AP total. The Bartokk did not expect you to move in close, and is not prepared for your attack. You strike and he collapses to the floor. If one of the Bartokks remains undefeated, go back to "Roll the 20-dice again for your new roll#" and repeat. When both assassins are defeated, you may proceed.

> *If your new adventure# is less than 16,* subtract the difference from your AP total. Although wounded, the savage Bartokk continues to fight. Go back to "Roll the 20-

dice again for your new roll#" and repeat. When both Bartokks are felled by your weapon, you may proceed.

For all you know, more Bartokks are on their way. You look inside the lift tube shaft. On the inner wall of the shaft, a maintenance ladder offers the possibility for ascent. Glancing back at the nursery, you see a flatboard repulsorlift scooter. The small scooter was designed for a child, but if it can support your weight, you might be able to use it to fly up the lift tube shaft to Level 58. The emergency stairwell presents a third option.

To reach Level 58 of the Science Service tower, choose to climb up the lift tube shaft, fly on the small repulsorlift scooter (or without the scooter, if flight is one of your talents), or run up the emergency stairwell.

To climb up the lift tube shaft: Roll the 10-dice to grab hold of the maintenance ladder. Your roll# + your strength# is your adventure#.

If your adventure# is equal to or more than 7, add the difference + 5 to your AP total. Despite the hazardous climb, you quickly scale the ladder to Level 58 and reach an access door. You may proceed.

If your adventure# is less than 7, subtract the difference from your AP total. The ladder is coated with grease and you can't keep your grip on it. Proceed to fly (below).

To fly: Roll the 20-dice to pilot the scooter up the shaft to Level 58. If flight is one of your talents, you do not need the scooter, and your roll# + your strength# + your stealth# + 3 is your roll#. If flight is not one of your talents, your roll# + your navigation# + your skill# is your adventure#.

If your adventure# is equal to or more than 14, add the difference + 6 to your AP total. Even though the repulsorlift scooter was designed for a child, it supports your weight and responds to your commands. Balancing on the scooter, you rise rapidly up through the shaft until you reach Level 58, where you find an access door. You may proceed.

If your adventure# is less than 14, subtract 5 AP from your AP total. You have some difficulty lifting off. If you tried using your flight ability, you will now have to use the scooter. You try to recalibrate the repulsorlift thrust to support your weight. Roll the 20-dice again for your new roll#. Your new roll# + your navigation# + your skill# + 1 is your new adventure#.

If your new adventure# is equal to or more than 14, add the difference to your AP total. The scooter lifts off, carrying you up the shaft to an access door at Level 58. You may proceed.

If your new adventure# is less than 14, subtract the difference from your AP total. You are too large to ride the child-sized repulsorlift scooter. Proceed to run up the emergency stairwell (below).

To run up the emergency stairwell: Roll the 10-dice to make your way up to Level 58 by the stairs. Your roll# + your stealth# + your strength# is your adventure#.

If your adventure# is equal to or more than 8, add the difference + 5 to your AP total. You race up the dark stairwell, quickly reaching an access door to Level 58. You may proceed.

If your adventure# is less than 8, subtract the difference from your AP total. You stumble in the darkened stairwell. Go back to "Roll the 10-dice to make your way up" and repeat.

When you have reached the access door to Level 58, you may proceed.

You have reached Level 58, but the access door is sealed. Fortunately, the locking mechanism is on your side of the door, and the lock does not look complicated. To open the access door, choose to hot-wire the lock or use your weapon.

To hot-wire the lock: Roll the 20-dice to use your unlocking skills to open the access door. Your roll# + your knowledge# + your skill# is your adventure#.

If your adventure# is equal to or more than 13, add the difference + 3 to your AP total. You open the lock with ease. The access door opens, and you may proceed.

If your adventure# is less than 13, subtract 7 AP from your AP total. You touch the lock and accidentally trigger a loud alarm. The deafening blare nearly causes you to fall down the lift tube shaft. Before you open the lock, you must turn off the alarm. Roll the 20-dice again for your new roll#. Your new roll# + your skill# is your new adventure#.

If your new adventure# is equal to or more than 11, add the difference to your AP total. Go back to "Roll the 20-dice to use your unlocking skills" and repeat. When you have successfully opened the access door, you may proceed.

If your new adventure# is less than 11, subtract the difference from your AP total. You manage to turn off the loud alarm, but you are unable to open the lock. Proceed to use your weapon (below).

To use your weapon: Choose your weapon. Roll the 10-dice to target the access door. Your roll# + your weaponry# + your weapon's close-range# is your adventure#.

If your adventure# is equal to or more than 9, add the difference + 5 to your AP total. You carve a hole clear through the access door. You may proceed.

If your adventure# is less than 9, subtract the difference from your AP total. You forgot to activate your weapon. Go back to "Roll the 10-dice to target the access door" and repeat. When you have made it through the access door, you may proceed.

You enter Level 58. Like the nursery fifty-one floors below, all the lights are off.

An Academy security droid is stationed next to the northeast lift tube. "You are not authorized to enter this level," the security droid states. "Command received from Level seven . . . all organic life-forms must evacuate the building."

You ignore the droid's directive, explaining you are here to search for Teela Panjarra.

"Teela Panjarra is in the care of Chief Scientist Frexton," the droid replies. "Now, I will direct you to the nearest exit."

You stand your ground and ask if Frexton is still on Level 58.

The droid quickly reaches out to grab your arm. "You must leave immediately."

The Academy security droid may be merely following orders, but you sense he is deliberately not answering your questions. It's possible he is acting under direct orders from the scheming Chief Scientist.

You cannot allow the menacing droid to prevent you from finding Teela Panjarra. To get past the security droid, choose to send the droid to Level 7 (using Power), switch off the droid, or combat the droid.

To send the droid to Level 7 (using Power): Roll the 20-dice to tell the droid there was an attack on Level 7, and that the Level 7 security droid was destroyed. You need to convince the droid that he's needed more on Level 7 than on Level 58. Your roll# + your Power# + your Power's mid-resist# + your charm# is your adventure#.

If your adventure# is equal to or more than 14, add the difference + 7 to your AP total. The droid races down the emergency stairwell to Level 7, and you may proceed.

If your adventure# is less than 14, subtract the difference from your AP total. The security droid suspects you might be responsible for the attack on Level 7. He grabs your arm and tells you that you are under arrest. He plans to escort you to a nearby detention cell. Proceed to switch off the droid or combat the droid (below).

*Note: This counts as one of three Power uses you are allowed on this adventure.

To switch off the droid: Roll the 10-dice to reach around the security droid's back and punch his deactivation switch. Your roll# + your stealth# + your skill# is your adventure#.

If your adventure# is equal to or more than 8, add the difference + 7 to your AP total. Not many people know it's so easy to switch off Academy security droids. Your knowledge and skill have served you well. The droid shuts down, and you may proceed.

If your adventure# is less than 8, subtract the difference from your AP total. You had no idea that this particular Academy security droid was designed without a manual deactivation switch. The annoyed droid tightens his grip on your arm. Proceed to combat the droid (below).

To combat the droid: Roll the 20-dice to hurl the droid down the emergency stairwell. If defense is one of your talents, your roll# + your strength# + 1 is your adventure#. If defense is not one of your talents, your roll# + your strength# is your adventure#.

If your adventure# is equal to or more than 12, add the difference + 5 to your AP total. You grab the security droid's forearm and twist your body, using the droid's own weight against him. The droid crashes down the emergency stairwell. You may proceed.

If your adventure# is less than 12, subtract 6 AP from your AP total. The surefooted droid regains his balance before you can throw him down the emergency stairwell. You will have to use a weapon against the droid. Choose your weapon. Roll the 20-dice again for your new roll#. Your new roll# + your weaponry# + your weapon's close-range# + 1 is your new adventure#.

If your new adventure# is equal to or more than 14, add the difference to your AP total. The menacing security droid is reduced to scrap metal by your weapon. You may proceed.

If your new adventure# is less than 14, subtract the difference from your AP total. The security droid is a surprisingly competent fighter and resists your attack. Go back to "Roll the 20-dice again for your new roll#" and repeat. When you have defeated the security droid, you may proceed.

Now that the Academy security droid is out of the way, you proceed into the lobby. On a wall next to a reception desk, a map reveals there are ten different research laboratories on Level 58. Each lab is represented by a color-coded rectangle. If you press a rectangle, a monitor will display a readout of the respective lab's purpose and contents. You must find out which laboratory contains Teela Panjarra.

To find out which laboratory contains Teela Panjarra: Roll the 10-dice to determine which labs you enter. Your roll# is your adventure#.

If your adventure# is 1 or 2: Subtract 1 AP from your AP total. You see two empty laboratories on the monitor. Roll again.

If your adventure# is 3 or 4: Subtract 3 AP from your AP total. The monitor displays two labs that are being cleaned by maintenance droids. There aren't any humans in either lab. Roll again.

If your adventure# is 5 or 6: The monitor displays two laboratories. Although you don't see any sign of an infant on the monitor, data indicates that a six-month-old female named Teela Panjarra is in one of the two labs. Add 40 AP to your AP total. You have located Teela Panjarra, and you may proceed.

If your adventure# is 7 or 8: Subtract 2 AP from your AP total. You see two hydroponic laboratories that are still under construction. The only evident life-forms within these two labs are plants. Roll again.

If your adventure# is 9 or 10: The monitor displays two laboratories that share common doors with the lab that contains Teela Panjarra. Add 20 AP to your AP total. You may proceed.

You go to the research laboratory that contains Teela Panjarra and peer inside the dark chamber. The lab is a long, deep room, dimly illuminated by the city light that seeps through a tinted picture window. Looking outside, you see starships flying to and from the Academy Spaceport.

Your eyes adjust to the darkness and you scan the lab. Electrical equipment is set up on a thick plastoid table. Hundreds of chemical vials are neatly displayed upon a series of wall-mounted shelves. Below the window, you see a dispersal canister for destroying lab waste and a portable fusion furnace for power generation.

Suddenly, the silhouette of a tall, slender man wearing a laboratory tunic moves in front of the picture window. The man is transferring something that looks like a bundled sack from a shallow rectangular tray into a medium-sized box. Despite the darkness, you recognize the box as a Live

Organism Comfort Conveyor (or LOCC), a contraption used to transport animals during interstellar journeys.

You quietly reach for the emergency glow rod on your belt. As soon as the slender man closes the lid on the conveyor, you activate the glow rod. Instantly, Chief Scientist Frexton is caught in the rod's bright light, and he throws a hand up over his eyes. A small transparent viewport built into the side of the conveyor reveals the bundled sack is in fact an infant swaddled in a pale gray fabric.

Teela Panjarra is humanoid. Her eyes are closed, and she appears to be sound asleep.

Keeping your voice calm, you command, "Surrender at once, Frexton."

"Security!" Frexton yelps as he squints into the glow rod's light. "Security! Get here at once!"

You begin to inform the scientist that the security droid cannot help him.

Before you can complete your sentence, the Chief Scientist draws a concealed blaster from his lab tunic. He raises the blaster fast and prepares to fire at you.

You want to defeat Frexton, but you don't want to cause any accidental harm to Teela Panjarra. To make Frexton release the blaster, choose to use Power, throw your glow rod at his blaster, or use your weapon to deflect the Chief Scientist's blaster fire.

To use Power*: Choose your Force Movement Power (you must be a Jedi to use this). Roll the 20-dice to disarm Frexton. Your roll# + your power# + 2 is your adventure#.

If your adventure# is equal to or more than 15, add the difference + 10 to your AP total. The blaster flies out of Frexton's hand and shatters against the wall. You may proceed.

If your adventure# is less than 15, subtract the difference from your AP total. Your mind is clouded by your anger at the Chief Scientist, and you are unable to use the Force. Proceed to throw your glow rod at his blaster (below) or use your weapon to deflect his fire (next page).

*NOTE: This counts as one of three Power uses you are allowed on this adventure.

To throw your glow rod at his blaster: Roll the 20-dice to hurl the glow rod. If targeting is one of your talents, your roll# + your strength# + 3 is your adventure#. If targeting is not one of your talents, your roll# + your strength# + 1 is your adventure#.

If your adventure# is equal to or more than 14, add the difference + 10 to your AP total. The glow rod cracks against Frexton's knuckles, causing him to drop the blaster. The fallen firearm skitters across the lab floor and slides under a heavy cabinet. Frexton cannot reach his lost blaster, and you may proceed.

If your adventure# is less than 14, subtract the difference from your AP total. Your throw is off, and you miss Frexton. Proceed to use your weapon to deflect the Chief Scientist's blaster fire (below).

To use your weapon to deflect the Chief Scientist's blaster fire: Choose your weapon. As you draw your weapon, Frexton fires his blaster. Roll the 20-dice to target the oncoming energy bolt. If defense is one of your talents, your roll# + your weaponry# + your weapon's mid-range# + 1 is your adventure#. If defense is not one of your talents, your roll# + your weaponry# + your weapon's mid-range# is your adventure#.

If your adventure# is equal to or more than 15, add the difference to your AP total. You use your weapon to slam the energy bolt back at the Chief Scientist. The bolt strikes his blaster, and he drops the ruined firearm. You may proceed.

If your adventure# is less than 15, subtract 6 AP from your AP total. Your weapon does not activate and you must dodge the fired energy bolt. Roll the 20-dice again for your new roll#. Your new roll# + your stealth# + 1 is your new adventure#.

If your new adventure# is equal to or more than 10, add the difference to your AP total. The energy bolt misses you and strikes the wall. Frexton prepares to fire again. Go back to "Roll the 20-dice to target the oncoming energy bolt" and repeat. When you have knocked the blaster from Frexton's hand, you may proceed.

If your new adventure# is less than 10, subtract the difference from your AP total. The shot grazes your arm — subtract 1 from your strength# for the rest of the adventure. Frexton prepares to fire again. Go back to "Roll the 20-dice to target the oncoming energy bolt" and repeat.

Frexton curses as his blaster smashes to the floor, ruined. You are about to reach for the LOCC containing the sleeping Teela Panjarra when you are distracted by movement outside the tinted window. Rising from a lower level, a wide window-washing drone rolls on magnetic treads up the tower's inclined exterior. On the drone's broad back stand two Bartokk assassins and a pair of X10-D draft droids. It's possible the Bartokks were drawn to the window because of the light from your glow rod.

Both Bartokks hold X10-D remote-control devices in their lower hands. With their upper limbs, one Bartokk operates the window-washing drone while the other fires a shoulder-mounted Squib battering ram, unleashing a powerful burst of alternating energy pulsations, and shattering the transparisteel window.

Frexton ducks behind a cabinet. Some of the transparisteel shrapnel strikes the lab's utility wall and punctures a plastoid plumbing hose, causing water to spray out all over the floor. Teela Panjarra is shielded from the shrapnel and water by her protective LOCC.

One of the two Bartokks wears a vocabulator. "Nobody movessss!" he hisses.

As the two Bartokks leap into the room, the Chief Scientist cowers behind the cabinet. The Bartokk assassins ignore the cringing scientist and focus their attention on the weapons in your belt.

"Brave warrior, are you?" asks the vocabulator-equipped Bartokk. "We'll see how tough you are."

The two Bartokks adjust their X10-D remote control devices, and the X10-D draft droids raise their extendable loader arms and lurch toward you. Before you can pursue the Chief Scientist, you must stop the assassins and their droids.

Water from the punctured plumbing hose has formed a large puddle in the middle of the lab. The Bartokks are standing in the puddle. You might be able to use the electrical equipment on the plastoid table to combat both Bartokks at once. If you defeat the Bartokks first, they won't be able to control the X10-Ds anymore, so the droids will also be defeated. If you fight the X10-Ds, you will still have to contend with the two Bartokks.

Choose to combat both Bartokks at once, combat one Bartokk at a time, or fight the two X10-D draft droids.

To combat both Bartokks at once: Roll the 20-dice. If strategy is one of your talents, your roll# + your strength# + your skill# + 1 is your adventure#. If strategy is not one of your talents, your roll# + your strength# + your skill# is your adventure#.

If your adventure# is equal to or more than 14, add the difference + 8 to your AP total. You push the electrical equipment off the table. It crashes onto the watery puddle, sending a massive electric jolt through the two insectoid assassins. The Bartokks appear to be frozen by the incredible shock, and the X10-Ds cease their movement. You may proceed.

If your adventure# is less than 14, subtract the difference from your AP total. The electrical equipment is not charged. The equipment crashes onto the wet floor but with no effect on the Bartokks. Proceed to combat one Bartokk at a time (below).

To combat one Bartokk at a time: Choose your weapon. Roll the 20-dice to go for the nearest assassin. Your roll# + your weaponry# + your weapon's mid-range# is your adventure#.

If your adventure# is equal to or more than 15, add the difference + 5 to your AP total. You easily defeat the nearest Bartokk. To attack the second Bartokk, go back to "Roll the 20-dice" and repeat. When you have defeated both Bartokks, they are no longer able to operate the remote-controlled X10-Ds, and you may proceed.

If your adventure# is less than 15, subtract 7 AP from your AP total. The Bartokk puts up a vicious fight, and you realize you must move closer to defeat him. Roll the 20-dice again for your new roll#. Your new roll# + your weaponry# + your weapon's close-range# is your new adventure#.

> *If your new adventure# is equal to or more than 15*, add the difference to your AP total. The Bartokk is defeated. If you have defeated both Bartokks, they are no longer in control of the X10-Ds. The two droids are motionless, and you may proceed. If there is still one Bartokk remaining, go back to "Roll the 20-dice again for your new roll#" and repeat.

> *If your new adventure# is less than 15*, subtract the difference from your AP total. Although you might have defeated one Bartokk, you have failed to defeat both of them. If both Bartokks remain undefeated,

each is still in control of an X10-D draft droid. If you defeated one Bartokk, the other Bartokk snatches the remote-control device from his partner's claws so he can operate both X10-Ds. The two droids charge at you. Proceed to fight the two X10-D draft droids (below).

To fight the two X10-D draft droids: Roll the 20-dice to knock the droids to the floor. If defense is one of your talents, your roll# + your skill# + your strength# is your adventure#. If defense is not one of your talents, your roll# + your strength# is your adventure#.

If your adventure# is equal to or more than 13, add the difference + 8 to your AP total. You push one droid into the other, and they both stumble and crash into the Bartokks. The droids' circuitry sends off deadly sparks. The Bartokks are defeated, and you may proceed.

If your adventure# is less than 13, subtract 7 AP from your AP total. You need to use more strength to knock over the droids. Roll the 20-dice again for your new roll#. Your new roll# + your strength# + 3 is your new adventure#.

If your new adventure# is equal to or more than 14, add the difference to your AP total. The droids crash into the Bartokks. The droids' circuitry sends off deadly sparks. You may proceed.

If your new adventure# is less than 14, subtract the difference from your AP total. The droids dodge your attack. Go back to "Roll the 20-dice again for your new roll#" and repeat. After you have knocked over the droids and both Bartokks are defeated, you may proceed.

The frightened Chief Scientist Frexton whimpers from behind the cabinet. You look at the LOCC and are amused to see that Teela Panjarra is still fast asleep in the protective container.

One of the Bartokks twitches on the floor. Somehow still alive, the fiendish assassin looks up at you and hisses through his vocabulator. He is mortally wounded, but he might live long enough for you to interrogate him. If you find out the nature of the Bartokks' murderous assignment, you might have a better chance of stopping any other X10-Ds that might be carrying plasma bombs.

On a rack of chemicals, you find a vial of Bavo Six truth serum. The wounded Bartokk wears a vocabulator, and you might be able to use the truth serum to make him reveal the assassins' secret plan.

To learn why the Bartokks have come to Corulag, choose to use Power or use Bavo Six truth serum.

To use Power*: Choose your Persuasion Power. Roll the 20-dice to make the Bartokk tell you about his assignment on Corulag. Your roll# + your Power# + your Power's mid-resist# + 1 is your adventure#.

If your adventure# is equal to or more than 11, add the difference + 20 to your AP total. The Bartokk is unable to resist your power, and tells you of the assassins' plan to use six X10-D draft droids to plant three plasma bombs in the Science Service tower, then blow up Corulag Academy. You may proceed.

If your adventure# is less than 11, subtract the difference from your AP total. Despite his wounds, the Bartokk resists your power and refuses to tell you about his mission. Proceed to use Bavo Six truth serum (next page).

*NOTE: This counts as one of three Power uses you are allowed on this adventure.

To use Bavo Six truth serum: Roll the 10-dice to give Bavo Six to the murderous assassin. Your roll# + your knowledge# + your skill# is your adventure#.

If your adventure# is equal to or more than 8, add the difference + 20 to your AP total. According to the Bartokk, the assassins plan to use six X10-D draft droids to plant three plasma bombs in the Science Service tower, then blow up Corulag Academy. You may proceed.

If your adventure# is less than 8, subtract the difference from your AP total. The Bartokk mentions something about blowing up the Academy — but that's all he'll say.

The wounded Bartokk's bulbous eyes seem to flex in his insectoid skull. Before you can find out who hired the assassins to destroy the Academy, the vile creature clicks his mandibles and exhales his last foul breath.

The Bartokk's X10-D remote-control device slips out of his lifeless claw and clatters on the floor. You suspect the device might be of use against the other X10-Ds, so you pick it up and secure it to your belt.

"Is it true?" asks the frightened Chief Scientist Frexton. "Are those creatures really going to blow up the entire Academy?"

You examine the two fallen X10-Ds. Without telling Frexton that one of the three bombs is no longer a concern, you carefully open the panels on the droids' chests. Just as you experienced on Level 7, one of the droids contains a plasma bomb.

Suddenly, two grappling hooks sail through the open window. Both hooks are tied off to climbing cables. The cables are drawn taut and the hooks sink into the base of the windowsill.

You fix your eyes on Frexton and tell him not to move. The fearful Frexton ducks back behind the cabinet.

You move to the window and glance down. Gripping the lines, two Bartokks pull themselves up to Level 58 from a balcony below.

There's only one way the Bartokks could have known where to look for you. The Bartokk who told you about the plan to destroy the Academy must have sent a telepathic communication to his comrades. That would also explain the way his eyes appeared to flex before he stopped breathing.

If the two Bartokks reach Level 58, they'll do whatever they can to recover their plasma bomb. They won't hesitate to eliminate everyone in the room. By using the X10-D remote you recovered, you might be able to combat the Bartokks with the droid that doesn't contain a bomb.

To prevent the two Bartokks from entering the laboratory, choose to pull the grappling hooks from the windowsill, sever the climbing cables, or command the X10-D to jump out the window.

To pull the grappling hooks from the windowsill: Roll the 10-dice to yank the hooks out from under the sill. Your roll# + your strength# + 3 is your adventure#.

If your adventure# is equal to or more than 9, add the difference + 15 to your AP total. Using all your strength, you pull the hooks out from the sill and let go of them. The hooks go sailing out the window and the two Bartokks smash hard against the balcony below. You glance out the window to note that neither Bartokk is moving. You may proceed.

If your adventure# is less than 9, subtract the difference from your AP total. The hooks are deeply embedded into the sill and you are unable to release them. Proceed to sever the climbing cables (below) or command the X10-D to jump out the window (next page).

To sever the climbing cables: Choose your weapon. Roll the 10-dice to target the cables. Your roll# + your weaponry# + your weapon's close-range# is your adventure#.

If your adventure# is equal to or more than 9, add the difference + 15 to your AP total. Your expert aim neatly cuts both climbing cables at the same time. While the grappling hooks remain anchored below the sill, the cut cables whip out the window. The Bartokks tumble down the exterior of the Science Service tower until they slam into the lower balcony. The two Bartokks are defeated, and you may proceed.

If your adventure# is less than 9, subtract the difference from your AP total. The climbing cables are made of molecularly reinforced line, and you are unable to cut through them. Proceed to command the X10-D to jump out the window (next page).

To command the X10-D to jump out th
window: Roll the 20-dice to use the remote
control device to direct the X10-D. Your roll# ·
your skill# + 2 is your adventure#.

If your adventure# is equal to or more tha
14, add the difference + 15 to your AP tota
Using the remote-control device, you maneu
ver the X10-D to step up to the window an
leap. Falling through the air, the mindles
droid slams into the two Bartokks, tearin
them from their climbing cables. The droi
carries the pair of assassins all the way dow
the side of the tower until they crash into th
walkway. The Bartokks are defeated, and yo
may proceed.

If your adventure# is less than 14, subtract
AP from your AP total. You fumble with th
remote control and are not able to make th
droid step over the windowsill. The two Ba
tokks leap over the sill and enter the labora
tory! Fortunately, you think you've figure
out how to operate the remote-control devic
Roll the 20-dice again for your new roll#
Your new roll# + your skill# + 1 is your nev
adventure#.

If your new adventure# is equal to or more
than 11, add the difference to your AP total. The two Bartokks prepare to attack,

unaware that you control the X10-D draft droid. You make the droid grab hold of the two assassins. Despite their strength and agility, the Bartokks are no match for the mindless droid. The Bartokks are defeated, and you may proceed.

If your new adventure# is less than 11, subtract the difference from your AP total. The remote-control device jams! Go back to "Roll the 20-dice again for your new roll#" and repeat. When you have successfully used the X10-D to defeat the two Bartokks, you may proceed.

Having defeated the two Bartokks, you return your attention to the plasma bomb within the X10-D draft droid. While you are removing the bomb from the droid's torso, Chief Scientist Frexton makes his move. He grabs the LOCC by its handle and runs through a triangular doorway.

You hear Frexton slip through the door and realize you should have subdued him when you had the chance. Although he has Teela Panjarra, you must get rid of the plasma bomb before you pursue the Chief Scientist.

Fortunately, the laboratory offers two

options to get rid of the bomb quickly. Choose to drop the bomb into the waste dispersal canister or place the bomb in the fusion furnace.

To drop the bomb into the waste dispersal canister: Roll the 10-dice to disintegrate the bomb by using the canister's contained fusion reactor. Your roll# + your skill# + your stealth# is your adventure#.

If your adventure# is equal to or more than 8, add the difference + 5 to your AP total. The plasma bomb disintegrates inside the dispersal canister, and you may proceed.

If your adventure# is less than 8, subtract the difference from your AP total. The dispersal canister is out of energy and does not operate. Proceed to place the bomb in the fusion furnace (below).

To place the bomb in the fusion furnace: Roll the 20-dice to overload the bomb with energy. Your roll# + your skill# + 1 is your adventure#.

If your adventure# is equal to or more than 13, add the difference + 5 to your AP total. The plasma bomb's components are fused by the energy overload. The geodesic-shaped weapon is nothing but scrap. You may proceed.

If your adventure# is less than 13, subtract 7 AP from your AP total. A warning light flashes on the fusion furnace. The plasma bomb has become unstable and will explode unless you adjust the energy flow of the fusion furnace. Roll the 20-dice again for your new roll#. Your new roll# + your skill# + 2 is your new adventure#.

> *If your new adventure# is equal to or more than 13*, add the difference to your AP total. The adjusted energy flow zaps the plasma bomb and fries its components. The bomb is destroyed, and you may proceed.

> *If your new adventure# is less than 13*, subtract the difference from your AP total. The warning light is still flashing. Mere seconds are left before the plasma bomb detonates! Go back to "Roll the 20-dice again for your new roll#" and repeat. When you have destroyed the bomb's components, you may proceed.

You have successfully destroyed the second plasma bomb. Add 25 AP to your AP total.

You race after Frexton, but he has activated an energy field that seals off the triangular doorway. The energy field is invisible, allowing you to peer through the doorway and into the next chamber. Frexton has entered an adjoining laboratory that is used for hydroponic research. The laboratory is filled with water tanks that contain large alien plants. Frexton is also visible at the far end of the room, carrying the conveyor as he walks toward a lift tube.

A wide window is angled over a row of water tanks. The window is open, allowing fresh night air into the lab. The open window reminds you that the Bartokks rose to Level 58 on a window-washing drone. You might be able to steer the window-washing drone on a horizontal course, then enter the hydroponics lab through its open window. Another option is to go directly through the lab wall. Your own weapon or the Bartokks' Squib battering ram should enable you to accomplish this feat.

You must pursue Frexton and rescue Teela Panjarra. To enter the lab, choose to ride the window-washing drone, use the Squib battering ram, or use your weapon.

To ride the window-washing drone: Roll the 10-dice to step through the shattered window and onto the drone. If navigation is one of your talents, your roll# + your navigation# + 2 is your adventure#. If navigation is not one of your talents, your roll# + your navigation# is your adventure#.

If your adventure# is equal to or more than 8, add the difference + 5 to your AP total. Outside the Science Service tower, you navigate the drone over to the open window that leads to the hydroponics lab. You may proceed.

If your adventure# is less than 8, subtract 5 AP from your AP total. You throw the wrong switch and the window-washing drone descends rapidly along the tower's inclined exterior. You must gain control of the drone and navigate it back up to the open window of the hydroponics lab. Roll the 10-dice again for your new roll#. Your new roll# + your navigation# + your skill# is your new adventure#.

If your new adventure# is equal to or more than 8, add the difference to your AP total. The drone moves diagonally up until you reach the open window of the hydroponics lab. You may proceed.

If your new adventure# is less than 8, subtract the difference from your AP total. You manage to guide the drone back up to the shattered window, but are unable to move sideways to the open window of the hydroponics lab. You reenter the lab that contains the fallen Bartokks and X10-Ds. Proceed to use the Squib battering ram (below) or your weapon (next page).

To use the Squib battering ram: Roll the 10-dice to pick up the Bartokk's rammer and target the wall that separates you from the hydroponics lab. Your roll# + your skill# is your adventure#.

If your adventure# is equal to or more than 7, add the difference + 5 to your AP total. You fire the battering ram and the wall crashes down, enabling you to walk over the rubble and into the hydroponics lab. You may proceed.

If your adventure# is less than 7, subtract the difference from your AP total. The Squib battering ram has been modified so it can only be fired by Bartokks. Because you are not a Bartokk, the battering ram is useless. Proceed to use your weapon (below).

To use your weapon: Choose your weapon. Roll the 20-dice to target the laboratory wall. Your roll# + your weaponry# + your weapon's mid-range# is your adventure#.

If your adventure# is equal to or more than 15, add the difference + 5 to your AP total. The wall yields to your weapon, and you create a hole that allows you to enter the hydroponics lab. You may proceed.

If your adventure# is less than 15, subtract the difference from your AP total. The wall is thicker than you'd imagined. You must recalibrate your weapon and step closer. Roll the 20-dice again for your new roll#. Your new roll# + your weaponry# + your weapon's close-range# is your new adventure#.

If your new adventure# is equal to or more than 14, add the difference to your AP total. In seconds, your recalibrated weapon creates a hole in the wall, giving you access to the hydroponics lab. You may proceed.

If your new adventure# is less than 14, subtract the difference from your AP total. Go back to "Roll the 20-dice again for your new roll#" and repeat. When you manage to carve or blast through the laboratory wall, you may proceed.

Wasting no time, you leap into the hydroponics laboratory. Frexton gasps at the sight of you, and clenches the LOCC against his chest.

"You can't have the child!" Frexton shouts. "My research depends on her. She belongs to the Academy!"

You tell him that the girl is not a piece of property. He must surrender.

Frexton ignores your order and runs behind a barrel-shaped transparisteel water tank. The tank contains an immense purple plant. The plant's thick leaf-covered vines extend out of the top of the tank and brush the ceiling before curving out to dangle down to the white-tiled floor.

You push your way through the plant's leaves. Moving forward, you feel one of your legs become entangled by the plant's vines. Suddenly, you are yanked off the laboratory floor and raised toward the ceiling.

You have been captured by an alien plant. As you struggle against the vines, the plant positions you over the top of the water tank. Inside the tank, under the water's surface, you see the plant's central stalk widen to reveal a mouth filled with razor-sharp teeth. The stalk breaks the water's surface. Yellow foam spills out of the plant's mouth.

The plant is very, very hungry.

It is possible the alien plant possesses intelligence and that you can communicate with it. As frightening as the plant appears, it might not even be carnivorous. It is also possible that the plant is a mindless eating machine.

To escape the clutches of the alien plant, choose to use Power, ask the plant to release you, or use your weapon.

To use Power*: Choose your Attention Power, Confusion Power, or (if you are a Jedi) your Force Movement Power (it must allow you to compel the plant to release its grip). Roll the 20-dice to escape the plant's grasp. Your roll# + your Power# + your Power's mid-resist# is your adventure#.

If your adventure# is equal to or more than 12, add the difference + 10 to your AP total. The Force has influence over the alien plant.

Against its will, the plant releases you. You land on the laboratory floor and may proceed.

If your adventure# is less than 12, subtract the difference + 10 from your AP total. The plant tightens its hold and you are unable to focus. You are drawn closer to the plant's mouth. Proceed to ask the plant to release you (below) or use your weapon (next page).

*NOTE: This counts as one of three Power uses you are allowed on this adventure.

To ask the plant to release you: Roll the 10-dice to ask the creature to release you. If either communication or wisdom is one of your talents, your roll# + your charm# + 1 is your adventure#. If neither communication nor wisdom is one of your talents, your roll# + your charm# is your adventure#.

If your adventure# is equal to or more than 8, add the difference + 10 to your AP total. The plant is not only intelligent but also merciful. It apologizes to you for almost having eaten you, but the sightless creature mistook your scent for its evening meal. The plant lowers you to the floor, and you may proceed.

If your adventure# is less than 8, subtract the difference from your AP total. Three long yellow tongues extend from the plant's mouth. The plant licks its lips and is clearly looking forward to dinner. You are left with no choice but to use your weapon (below).

To use your weapon: Roll the 20-dice to target the vines that grip you. If defense is one of your talents, your roll# + your weaponry# + your weapon's close-range# + 1 is your adventure#. If defense is not one of your talents, your roll# + your weaponry# + your weapon's close-range# is your adventure#.

If your adventure# is equal to or more than 14, add the difference + 7 to your AP total. You sever the vines and the plant screeches as it releases you. You land on the laboratory floor and may proceed.

If your adventure# is less than 14, subtract 7 AP from your AP total. The plant puts up a furious battle, lashing out and snaring you with more vines. To free yourself from the plant, you must use your strength as well as your weapon. Roll the 20-dice again for your new roll#. Your new roll# + your strength# + your weaponry# + your weapon's close-range# is your new adventure#.

If your new adventure# is equal to or more than 15, add the difference to your AP total. The plant is minus over a dozen of its thick vines when it finally yields and drops you. You land on the floor and may proceed.

If your new adventure# is less than 15, subtract the difference from your AP total. The plant is determined to make a meal of you. Go back to "Roll the 20-dice again for your new roll#" and repeat. When you have defeated the carnivorous plant, you land on the floor and may proceed.

As you rise from the floor, the lift tube doors open. Frexton runs away from the barrel-shaped tank and jumps into the lift tube. You sprint after him, but the lift tube doors begin to slide shut. In desperation, you reach forward and wedge your hands into the sliding doors. You force the doors open, but the lift begins to descend before you can enter.

Braced within the doorway, you watch the lift drop into the shaft. A whirring sound from above causes you to look down and see a six-wheeled shaft maintenance droid. The bulky droid is not at all humanoid in appearance, and resembles a scaled-down tank. A small platform is positioned on the droid's back, just behind its cylindrical head. Following the lift, the maintenance droid is demagnetizing the lift guidance rail that's secured to the shaft wall.

To pursue Frexton, choose to leap on top of the descending lift, ride the shaft maintenance droid, or slide down the lift guidance rail.

To leap on top of the descending lift: Roll the 10-dice to jump onto the lift. Your roll# + your stealth# + your strength# is your adventure#.

If your adventure# is equal to or more than 9, add the difference to your AP total. You land on top of the lift without making a sound. You may proceed.

If your adventure# is less than 9, subtract the difference from your AP total. The lift is dropping too rapidly, and any attempt to jump would be hazardous. Proceed to ride the shaft maintenance droid (below).

To ride the shaft maintenance droid: Roll the 20-dice to step onto the droid's back. Your roll# + your stealth# is your adventure#.

If your adventure# is equal to or more than 11, add the difference to your AP total. You land on the droid's back and the machine continues its route, closely following the descending lift. You may proceed.

If your adventure# is less than 11, subtract 6 AP from your AP total. You land on the droid's back, and the droid comes to a sudden stop on the vertical rail. The droid turns its cylindrical head and stares at you with a single red photoreceptor. "You are not an authorized service technician," the droid says. "Explain your presence in this lift tube shaft." You must answer the droid, telling it that you're trying to rescue a hostage child within the descending lift. Roll the 20-dice again for your new roll#. Your new roll# + your charm# is your new adventure#.

If your new adventure# is equal to or more than 12, add the difference to your AP total. The droid believes you, and it activates its motor to race after the descending lift. You catch up with the lift, and you may proceed.

If your new adventure# is less than 12, subtract the difference from your AP total. The shaft maintenance droid suspects you are

trying to sabotage the lift, and says, "You
will come with me to the nearest security
droid." The droid begins to rise up the
shaft, away from the descending lift, and
you jump off its back. Proceed to slide
down the lift guidance rail (below).

To slide down the lift guidance rail: Roll
the 20-dice to grip the rail and slide to the descending lift. Your roll# + your strength# is your
adventure#.

*If your adventure# is equal to or more than
12*, add the difference to your AP total. The
rail is smooth, and you slide down through
the shaft faster than the lift itself. You land on
top of the lift, and you may proceed.

If your adventure# is less than 12, subtract 6
AP from your AP total. You grab hold of the
rail but your left sleeve snags on a piece of
protruding metal. Over your head, the maintenance droid descends, heading straight for
you. You must tear your sleeve free from the
protruding metal before you are slammed by
the droid. Roll the 20-dice again for your new
roll#. Your new roll# + your strength# + 2 is
your new adventure#.

*If your new adventure# is equal to or more
than 13*, add the difference to your AP to-

tal. You tear your sleeve free from the protruding metal and slide down to the top of the descending lift. You may proceed.

If your new adventure# is less than 13, subtract the difference from your AP total. You remain snagged, and the droid draws closer. Go back to "Roll the 20-dice again for your new roll#" and repeat. When you have torn your sleeve from the protruding metal and slid down to the lift, you may proceed.

You are on top of the lift when it comes to a sudden, jarring stop. By your estimate, the lift is somewhere between Levels 35 and 40. You'd thought Frexton might have been attempting to reach Level 1 or one of the Science Service tower's sub-levels, so you are surprised that the lift would stop so soon. You hunker down on top of the stalled lift and place your ear over the upper emergency access hatch. You hear the sound of the tube doors opening.

Then Frexton begins to scream.

You don't know why Frexton is screaming, but it's an easy guess that he's in trouble. He still has Teela Panjarra. You can't allow anything bad to happen to the Force-sensitive infant. You must enter the lift.

To enter the lift, choose to open the emergency access hatch or use your weapon.

To open the emergency access hatch: Roll the 10-dice to fling the hatch open. Your roll# + your skill# + your strength# is your adventure#.

If your adventure# is equal to or more than 8, add the difference + 10 to your AP total. The hatch swings open and you leap down into the lift cabin. You may proceed.

If your adventure# is less than 8, subtract the difference from your AP total. The lift's upper emergency access hatch is locked. Since Teela Panjarra is in danger, taking the time to hotwire the lock is not an option. Proceed to use your weapon (below).

To use your weapon: Choose your weapon. Roll the 20-dice to target the lift's upper emergency hatch. Your roll# + your weaponry# + your weapon's close-range# is your adventure#.

If your adventure# is equal to or more than 14, add the difference + 8 to your AP total. Using your weapon, you shear the hatch clear off the lift's top, then leap down through the open hole and into the lift cabin. You may proceed.

If your adventure# is less than 14, subtract 7 AP from your AP total. Your weapon has only loosened the lift's upper hatch. If you jump on top of the hatch, you should be able to force it open. Roll the 20-dice again for your new roll#. Your new roll# + your strength# + 2 is your new adventure#.

> *If your new adventure# is equal to or more than 14*, add the difference to your AP total. You crash down through the loosened hatch and land inside the lift cabin. You may proceed.

> *If your new adventure# is less than 14*, subtract the difference from your AP total. Your jump loosens the hatch even more, but you'll need to jump again. Go back to "Roll the 20-dice again for your new roll#" and repeat. When you have broken through the hatch and land inside the lift cabin, you may proceed.

From inside the lift cabin, you gaze through the open lift tube doors to see that you're on Level 32. According to a sign on the wall, Level 32 is devoted to aeronautic research and development.

"Get away from me!" Chief Scientist Frexton yells from outside the lift.

You step out of the lift cabin and the doors slide shut behind you. An antechamber leads directly to an aeronautic laboratory, where Academy scientists and engineers develop new repulsorlift systems. You see a tall, robotic figure standing in the entrance to the lab and almost mistake it for an X10-D before you realize it's just an unmanned bipedal servo-lifter. Like the X10-Ds, servo-lifters are used for moving heavy freight, but they are operated by a pilot instead of by remote control. The pilot has already fled. You duck behind the two-legged loading machine to peer inside the lab.

You see Frexton cowering against a wall, held at bay by a single X10-D draft droid. Numerous storage bins filled with starship engine parts are also evident, but there isn't any sign of the LOCC that contains Teela Panjarra. You don't see any Bartokks, but you know that they must be nearby if they are controlling the X10-D.

"Help!" Frexton shouts as the droid raises a metal claw and prepares to strike. Since this droid might contain the third plasma bomb, you must take care not to damage its torso.

To stop the X10-D, choose to use your remote-control device, commandeer the servo-lifter, or use your weapon.

To use your remote-control device: Roll the 20-dice to override the Bartokk's commands and seize control of the droid. Your roll# + your knowledge# + your skill# is your adventure#.

If your adventure# is equal to or more than 13, add the difference + 10 to your AP total. Using your remote-control device, you make the X10-D reach up and tear its own head from its body. A shower of sparks erupts from its neck socket, and the mindless droid keels over backward, crashing to the lab floor. The droid is disabled, and you may proceed.

If your adventure# is less than 13, subtract the difference from your AP total. You are unable to gain control of the X10-D. Proceed to commandeer the servo-lifter (below) or use your weapon (next page).

To commandeer the servo-lifter: Roll the 20-dice to climb onto the servo-lifter and activate the controls. Your roll# + your skill# + 2 is your adventure#.

If your adventure# is equal to or more than 13, add the difference + 10 to your AP total. Moving forward in the servo-lifter, you use its powerful mechanical arms to reach out and chop at the unprepared X10-D's head. The X10-D's head is torn from its shoulders and smashes into the wall. The droid's body teeters on its legs, then topples to the floor. You may proceed.

If your adventure# is less than 13, subtract 6 AP from your AP total. The droid turns its head to see you approach on the servo-lifter. The Bartokks now know your exact position! Roll the 20-dice again for your new roll#. Your new roll# + your skill# + 3 is your new adventure#.

If your new adventure# is equal to or more than 13, add the difference to your AP total. Before the unseen Bartokks can set the X10-D to attack, you quickly maneuver the servo-lifter's arms to tear the droid's head from its body. The droid's body collapses to the floor, and you may proceed.

If your new adventure# is less than 13, subtract the difference from your AP total. Under the remote control of the Bartokks, the droid bashes away at your servo-lifter until it breaks your machine's left leg. You leap down from the damaged servo-lifter and reach for your weapons belt. Proceed to use your weapon (below).

To use your weapon: Choose your weapon. Roll the 20-dice to aim for the droid. If targeting is one of your talents, your roll# + your skill# + your weaponry# + your weapon's mid-range# is your adventure#. If targeting is not one of your talents, your roll# + your weaponry# + your weapon's mid-range# is your adventure#.

If your adventure# is equal to or more than 15, add the difference + 10 to your AP total. You may proceed. The X10-D's head is shaved from its neck and smashes against the far wall. The droid's body walks in a complete circle before its knees buckle, and it crashes to the floor. You may proceed.

If your adventure# is less than 15, subtract 8 AP from your AP total. The X10-D seems to be prepared for your attack, and it forces you back into a corner of the lab. There's little room for movement in the corner, and you are unable to bring your weapon up to fight the X10-D. You must dive under the droid's legs to evade the droid. Roll the 20-dice again for your new roll#. Your new roll# + your stealth# + 2 is your new adventure#.

If your new adventure# is equal to or more than 13, add the difference to your AP total. You evade the droid, and come up fighting. Go back to "Roll the 20-dice to aim for the droid" and repeat. When you have separated the droid's head from its body, you may proceed.

If your new adventure# is less than 13, subtract the difference from your AP total. The X10-D really has you boxed into that corner. Go back to "Roll the 20-dice again for your new roll#" and repeat. When you have evaded the droid and removed its head, you may proceed.

Chief Scientist Frexton faints. You try to revive him, but he's out cold.

You kneel down over the fallen body of the decapitated X10-D. Opening a panel on the droid's chest, you discover the droid does not contain a plasma bomb.

Suddenly, bright overhead lights switch on, illuminating the entire aeronautics laboratory. You can now see the other areas of the lab that were previously cast in shadow.

Ten meters away from you, the LOCC is on the lab floor. The sixth X10-D draft droid has one foot firmly planted on top of it. Three Bartokk assassins are also in the lab. One Bartokk operates the X10-D remote-control device while the other two aim crossbows loaded with explosive-tipped arrows at your heart.

You've walked right into the Bartokks' trap.

One of the crossbow-wielding Bartokks wears a vocabulator. Clicking its mandibles, the Bartokk cautions, "If you make any sudden movement, the droid will crush the container and its contents."

You do not move. You know the Bartokk is serious.

"Our brothers on Level fifty-eight telepathically warned us of your position before they perished," the Bartokk continues. "We anticipated you would try to escape the tower, so we programmed all lifts to stop on this level. You have meddled with our assignment for the last time."

Your mind races, trying to plan your next move. You still possess the X10-D remote-control device that you took from the Bartokk in the laboratory, and you might be able to use it to override the control of the

X10-D that threatens to stomp the conveyor. You are confident you can reach your weapon before the Bartokks can fire their arrows, but the Bartokk who controls the X10-D is a more immediate concern. Hoping to buy time, you point out that the Bartokks will perish too if they detonate a plasma bomb.

The vocabulator-equipped Bartokk tilts his insectoid head toward a repulsorlift skiff parked next to a transport hatch. "We will leave the Science Service tower in our skiff and return to our starship. There is no place for you to run, warrior. We've sealed off this entire laboratory. We intend to leave you trapped within the tower. By the time the bomb detonates, we will be far away from Curamelle city. Now you will remove your weapons."

To prevent the X10-D from crushing the conveyor, you must deal with the Bartokk who controls the droid. To battle the first Bartokk, choose to use your X10-D remote-control device or your lightsaber.

To use your X10-D remote-control device: Roll the 10-dice to seize control of the

X10-D. If strategy is one of your talents, your roll# + your skill# + 2 is your adventure#. If strategy is not one of your talents, your roll# + your skill# is your adventure#.

If your adventure# is equal to or more than 8, add the difference + 15 to your AP total. Using the remote-control device, you seize control of the X10-D. You make the droid turn and attack his Bartokk controller. The X10-D pounces on the Bartokk, crushing both the assassin and its own remote control. The first of the three Bartokks is defeated, and you may proceed.

If your adventure# is less than 8, subtract the difference from your AP total. You cannot override the Bartokk's signal to control the X10-D. Proceed to use your lightsaber (below).

To use your lightsaber: Choose your lightsaber. Roll the 20-dice to target the Bartokk who operates the X10-D draft droid. If defense is one of your talents, your roll# + your weaponry# + your weapon's mid-range# + 2 is your adventure#. If defense is not one of your talents, your roll# + your weaponry# + your weapon's mid-range# is your adventure#.

If your adventure# is equal to or more than 15, add the difference to your AP total. You destroy both the Bartokk and his remote-control device. Collapsing to the floor, the Bartokk knocks the X10-D off balance, and the droid tumbles away from the conveyor. The fallen Bartokk's two comrades are amazed by your speed and fighting skills, yet they prepare to attack. You may proceed.

If your adventure# is less than 15, subtract 9 AP from your AP total. You destroyed the Bartokk's remote control device, and the X10-D collapses to the aeronautic lab floor, but the Bartokk is not injured. You'll have to move in closer to strike the Bartokk. Roll the 20-dice again for your new roll#. If defense is one of your talents, your new roll# + your weaponry# + your weapon's close-range# + 2 is your new adventure#. If defense is not one of your talents, your new roll# + your weaponry# + your weapon's close-range# is your new adventure#.

If your new adventure# is equal to or more than 15, add the difference to your AP total. The first Bartokk is quickly defeated, and you may proceed.

If your new adventure# is less than 15, subtract the difference from your AP total. The ferocious Bartokk repels your assault. Go back to "Roll the 20-dice again for your new roll#" and repeat. When you have defeated the first Bartokk, you may proceed.

You stand protectively in front of the conveyor that contains Teela Panjarra. The two crossbow-wielding Bartokks fire explosive-tipped arrows at you. Choose to use Power or use your weapon to deflect the explosive arrows, or choose to grab the LOCC and dodge the explosive arrows. If you catch the explosive arrows using Power, you will be able to use them against the Bartokks.

To use Power to deflect the explosive arrows*: Choose your Redirect Power or (if you are a Jedi) your Force Movement Power. Roll the 20-dice to deflect the oncoming arrows. Your roll# + your Power# + your Power's mid-resist# is your adventure#.

If your adventure# is equal to or more than 12, add the difference + 10 to your AP total. You knock the flying arrows out of the air. You now have the option of throwing them back. You may proceed.

If your adventure# is less than 12, subtract the difference from your AP total. The arrows are coming too fast. Proceed to use your weapon to deflect the explosive arrows (below) or grab the LOCC and dodge the explosive arrows (next page).

*Note: This counts as one of three Power uses you are allowed on this adventure.

To use your weapon to deflect the explosive arrows: Roll the 20-dice to target the oncoming arrows. Your roll# + your weaponry# + your weapon's far-range# is your adventure#.

If your adventure# is equal to or more than 16, add the difference + 10 to your AP total. You deflect the arrows before they can reach you. The arrows career into the walls of the aeronautics lab, exploding and spraying fragments of the walls all over the chamber. You and Teela Panjarra are unharmed. You may proceed.

If your adventure# is less than 16, subtract 4 AP from your AP total. You deflect the arrows — but then the Bartokk deflects them back at you. You must target them again. Roll the 20-dice again for your new roll#. Your new roll# + your weaponry# + your weapon's close-range# is your new adventure#.

If your new adventure# is equal to or more than 15, add the difference to your AP total. You strike at the oncoming arrows and they veer off into the walls. The explosive-tipped arrows detonate, but you and the sleeping Teela Panjarra are not injured. You may proceed.

If your new adventure# is less than 15, subtract the difference from your AP total. Quickly proceed to grab the LOCC and dodge the explosive arrows (below).

To grab the LOCC and dodge the explosive arrows: Roll the 10-dice to push the conveyor out of harm's way. Your roll# + your strength# + your stcalth# is your adventure#.

If your adventure# is equal to or more than 8, add the difference + 10 to your AP total. With incredible speed, you throw yourself onto the LOCC and push it away from the oncoming arrows. The arrows whiz past your legs and travel to the far end of the aeronautics lab. The arrows destroy the wall, but you and the sleeping Teela Panjarra are unharmed. You may proceed.

If your adventure# is less than 8, subtract the difference from your AP total. The LOCC is heavier than you anticipated, and you will have to use more strength. Roll the 10-dice

again for your new roll#. Your new roll# +
your strength# + your stealth# + 1 is your new
adventure#.

*If your new adventure# is equal to or more
than 8*, add the difference to your AP total.
The arrows nearly graze the back of your
skull as you push the LOCC to the side. The
arrows reach the end of the aeronautics lab
and explode, but you and Teela Panjarra
are not hurt. You may proceed.

If your new adventure# is less than 8, subtract the difference from your AP total. You
stumble against the LOCC and fall. Luckily,
the arrows fly over your head. You may
proceed.

The two Bartokks prepare to fire more
explosive-tipped arrows. Choose to combat both Bartokks at once using Power, or
combat them one at a time. If the explosive arrows landed at your feet (after you
deflected them with Power) you may also
choose to throw the explosive arrows at
the two Bartokks.

**To throw the explosive arrows at the
two Bartokks:** (The explosive arrows must

have been knocked from the air on page 83). Roll the 10-dice to fling the arrows back at the crossbow-wielding assassins. Your roll# + your strength# is your adventure#.

If your adventure# is equal to or more than 7, add the difference + 10 to your AP total. You hurl the arrows straight at the Bartokks. You score two direct hits. You may proceed.

If your adventure# is less than 7, subtract the difference from your AP total. The quick-reflexed Bartokks catch the arrows with their upper claws while their lower claws tense on their crossbow triggers. Proceed to combat the Bartokks one at a time (next page).

To combat the two Bartokks (using Power)*: Choose your Redirect Power or your Confusion Power. Roll the 20-dice to make the Bartokks train their crossbows at each other. Your roll# + your Power# + your Power's mid-resist# is your adventure#.

If your adventure# is equal to or more than 12, add the difference + 10 to your AP total. The two assassins aim at each other and fire their arrows. Both Bartokks are destroyed in the resulting explosion. You may proceed.

If your adventure# is less than 12, subtract 7 AP from your AP total. The Bartokks struggle against your effort to control their actions. You must draw on your extensive experience with the Force to overcome the murderous thoughts of the two assassins. Roll the 20-dice again for your new roll#. If either calm or wisdom is one of your talents, your new roll# + your knowledge# + your Power# + your Power's mid-resist# is your new adventure#. If neither calm nor wisdom is one of your talents, your new roll# + your Power# + your Power's mid-resist# is your new adventure#.

If your new adventure# is equal to or more than 15, add the difference to your AP total. You win the mental battle with the Bartokks, and the two assassins turn their weapons on each other. The two Bartokks are instantly eliminated, and you may proceed.

If your new adventure# is less than 15, subtract the difference from your AP total. The Bartokks will not bend to your will. Proceed to combat them one at a time (below).

*NOTE: This counts as one of three Power uses you are allowed on this adventure.

To combat the Bartokks one at a time: Choose your weapon. Roll the 20-dice to battle the crossbow-wielding assassins. If defense is one of your talents, your roll# + your weaponry# +

your weapon's mid-range# + 1 is your adventure#. If defense is not one of your talents, your roll# + your weaponry# + your weapon's mid-range# is your adventure#.

If your adventure# is equal to or more than 14, add the difference + 7 to your AP total. You may proceed. Moving faster than the Bartokks' multifaceted eyes can follow, you cut down the nearest Bartokk. Go back to "Roll the 20-dice to battle" and repeat. When you have defeated both assassins, you may proceed.

If your adventure# is less than 14, subtract 8 AP from your AP total. The Bartokk's own fighting skills almost match your own. To defeat the Bartokk, you must employ all your skills. Roll the 20-dice again for your new roll#. If defense is one of your talents, your new roll# + your skill# + your weaponry# + your weapon's mid-range# is your new adventure#. If defense is not one of your talents, your new roll# + your skill# + your weaponry# + your weapon's close-range# is your new adventure#.

If your new adventure# is equal to or more than 14, add the difference to your AP total. The Bartokk falls to your superior abilities in combat. If one Bartokk remains undefeated, go back to "Roll the 20-dice again for your new roll#" and repeat. When both assassins have been vanquished, you may proceed.

If your new adventure# is less than 14, subtract the difference from your AP total. The Bartokk is now minus one arm, and the injury only increases the ferocity of his attack. Go back to "Roll the 20-dice again for your new roll#" and repeat. When you have defeated the two Bartokks, you may proceed.

The three Bartokks and the two X10-D draft droids lie motionless on the floor under the bright lights of the aeronautics lab. Nearby, the unconscious Chief Scientist Frexton remains stretched out on the spot where he fainted.

You go to the conveyor and look through its small viewport. Miraculously, Teela Panjarra remains sound asleep, and has a faint smile on her lips.

For rescuing Teela Panjarra, reward yourself with 100 AP.

You step away from the conveyor and go to the sixth X10-D. Opening its chest plate, you find what you expected: the third plasma bomb. As you carefully remove the bomb from the droid, you see the Bartokks have taken an extreme precaution to prevent you from deactivating the explosive device.

Unlike the other two plasma bombs, the third bomb has a secured timer mechanism that has been set for a five-minute countdown. Any attempt to switch off the secured timer will cause the bomb to explode.

Since Bartokks communicate telepathically, the four surviving members of the hive must be aware they've lost the three Bartokks in the aeronautics lab. Now nothing prevents the remaining Bartokks from leaving Corulag.

You realize you are the only one who can get rid of the bomb and stop the Bartokks. Although it will be a dangerous mission, you dare not leave Teela Panjarra alone and undefended in the tower. You reluctantly decide to take the LOCC with you as well as the plasma bomb.

An experimental Academy fighter craft rests alongside the Bartokks' skiff near the transport hatch. Both the fighter craft and the skiff are equipped with laser cannons.

You must fly away from the tower.

To fly away from the tower: Choose your vehicle (it must be capable of flight). Roll the 10-dice to launch through the hatch and out of the aeronautics lab. Your roll# + your navigation# + your vehicle's speed# is your adventure#.

If your adventure# is equal to or more than 9, add the difference + 5 to your AP total. Accompanied by Teela Panjarra and the plasma bomb, you blast away from Level 32 of the Science Service tower. You may proceed.

If your adventure# is less than 9, subtract the difference from your AP total. Your chosen vehicle's engine stalls. Roll the 10-dice again for your new roll#. Your new roll# + navigation# + your skill# is your new adventure#.

If your new adventure# is equal to or more than 8, add the difference to your AP total. The vehicle blasts away from Level 32, and you may proceed.

If your new adventure# is less than 8, subtract the difference from your AP total. You forgot to release the inertial dampers. Go

> back to "Roll the 10-dice again for your
> new roll#" and repeat. When you have
> launched from the Science Service tower,
> you may proceed.

You soar away from the pyramidal Science Service tower and loop around to locate the stolen SoroSuub space yacht. The lights of Curamelle seem to flow past your vehicle like an illuminated wave. Searching for the space yacht, you angle toward the low-rise buildings across from the tower's nursery window on Level 7.

Then you see it. The SoroSuub space yacht is already moving up and away from its hiding place. You steer toward the space yacht, drawing closer until you are within thirty meters. Unfortunately, the Bartokks' sensors detect that you are following them.

A Bartokk appears on the stern and aims a disruptor rifle in your direction. The energy weapon is capable of unleashing a blast so powerful that it breaks down targets at the molecular level. To combat the Bartokk, choose to fire your vehicle's laser cannons, use your own weapon, or ram the Bartokk off the stern.

To fire your vehicle's laser cannons: Roll the 10-dice to target the Bartokk on the space yacht's stern. Your roll# + your skill# + your vehicle's weaponry# is your adventure#.

If your adventure# is equal to or more than 10, add the difference + 10 to your AP total. The Bartokk is defeated. You may proceed.

If your adventure# is less than 10, subtract the difference from your AP total. Your vehicle's weapons aren't online. Proceed to use your own weapon (below).

To use your own weapon: Choose your weapon. Roll the 20-dice to fly close to the space yacht and target the Bartokk. Your roll# + your navigation# + your weaponry# + your weapon's close-range# is your adventure#.

If your adventure# is equal to or more than 18, add the difference + 12 to your AP total. The Bartokk was unprepared for your attack, and falls to your weapon as you fly past the yacht's stern. You may proceed.

If your adventure# is less than 18, subtract the difference from your AP total. The Bartokk maintains heavy cover fire, preventing you from drawing close enough to use your weapon. Proceed to ram the Bartokk off the stern (below).

To ram the Bartokk off the stern: Roll the 20-dice to steer your vehicle on a collision course for the Bartokk. Your roll# + your navigation# + your vehicle's speed# is your adventure#.

If your adventure# is equal to or more than 15, add the difference to your AP total. Your vehicle comes within millimeters of the stern and slams into the Bartokk. The assassin is thrown from the space yacht and tumbles to its death. The Bartokk is defeated, and you may proceed.

If your adventure# is less than 15, subtract 8 AP from your AP total. While the Bartokk tries to aim the disruptor rifle at your vehicle, you realize you're about to crash into the stern. You must pull up and away from the yacht. Roll the 20-dice again for your new roll#. Your new roll# + your navigation# + your vehicle's stealth# is your new adventure#.

If your new adventure# is equal to or more than 14, add the difference to your AP total. You pull away from the yacht just in time, barely avoiding a violent crash. Maintaining your velocity, you swoop around for another try. Go back to "Roll the 20-dice to steer your vehicle on a collision course" and repeat. After you have rammed the assassin, you may proceed.

If your new adventure# is less than 14, subtract the difference from your AP total. Pull back harder, before you crash! Go back to "Roll the 20-dice again for your new roll#" and repeat. When you have veered away from the yacht, and successfully returned to slam the Bartokk with your vehicle, you may proceed.

As the SoroSuub space yacht races away from the city, you match speed with the yacht and land your vehicle on its open stern. You intend to plant the plasma bomb on the space yacht, then make your escape. Although there are barely two minutes left before the plasma bomb detonates, you want to be certain there aren't any innocent people on board the stolen yacht.

You leave Teela Panjarra in her LOCC, then carry the geodesic plasma bomb away from your vehicle and cross the yacht's aft deck. On the deck, you see the eliminated Bartokk's disruptor rifle lying intact near a guardrail.

You walk past a supply bulkhead and a hatch for an emergency escape pod. At the base of a curved, tubular air vent you peer through a viewport into the main cabin. Inside the cabin, three Bartokks operate the controls of the sleek vessel. They appear to be unaware of your presence on the yacht.

You must plant the plasma bomb. Choose to place the bomb in the supply bulkhead or toss the bomb into the tubular air vent.

To place the bomb in the supply bulkhead: Roll the 10-dice to raise the bulkhead hatch and deposit the plasma bomb. Your roll# + your stealth# is your adventure#.

If your adventure# is equal to or more than 7, add the difference + 5 to your AP total. The plasma bomb now rests among numerous ship-maintenance supplies. You lower the hatch, and may proceed.

If your adventure# is less than 7, subtract the difference from your AP total. The bulkhead's cheap plastoid handle snaps off of the hatch when you try to pull it and you notice that the entire bulkhead is made of a singular piece of durasteel. The bulkhead is a purely decorative extravagance on the luxury yacht. Proceed to toss the bomb into the tubular air vent (below).

To toss the bomb into the tubular air vent: Roll the 20-dice to hurl the plasma bomb up into the open vent. Your roll# + your strength# is your adventure#.

If your adventure# is equal to or more than 12, add the difference + 5 to your AP total. The plasma bomb flies directly into the air vent, and you may proceed.

If your adventure# is less than 12, subtract 6 AP from your AP total. The plasma bomb flies into the open vent, bounces off the vent's tubular interior, and rebounds out of the vent and back to you! You threw the bomb with too much strength. You must use more skill and less strength. Roll the 20-dice again for your new roll#. Your new roll# + your skill# + your strength# − 1 is your new adventure#.

If your new adventure# is equal to or more than 14, add the difference to your AP total. The plasma bomb sails into the air vent and lands within the yacht. You may proceed.

If your new adventure# is less than 14, subtract the difference from your AP total. Throwing the bomb into the air vent is more difficult that you'd expected. Go back to "Roll the 20-dice again for your new roll#" and repeat. When you have tossed the plasma bomb into the vent, you may proceed.

You race back across the deck and leap onto your vehicle. As you prepare for launch, you sense something is wrong. You look for Teela Panjarra's conveyor, and discover it's missing.

Without warning, the yacht's canopy shields rise swiftly and seal off the stern. You hear a chittering sound from the deck that causes you to turn.

A Bartokk Queen stands on the deck. In all your life, you have never before seen such a creature. She is taller than the average Bartokk, and her insectoid limbs display strong, flat muscles. You realize there can be only one explanation for her presence on the yacht: She must have decided to personally oversee the ill-fated assignment to Corulag. Except for a hand-held vocabulator, the Queen does not appear to be carrying any weapons. In her lower left claw, the Queen carries Teela Panjarra's LOCC.

Raising the vocabulator to her bulbous-eyed head, the Queen rasps, "Prepare to die, warrior."

As you step away from your vehicle, you tell her there's a bomb on the yacht and walk slowly toward the guardrail, under which lies the Bartokk disruptor rifle.

You tell her to surrender the child.

The Bartokk Queen laughs. Her gargled chittering sounds like it's laced with maggots. "Foolish warrior," she snarls. "For failing on our mission, we are prepared to die. You, on the other hand, have only managed to lock yourself up with us." The Queen extends her arm and crushes the vocabulator in her claw. She opens her claw, letting the broken bits fall to the stern's highly polished deck. Then she releases the LOCC, letting it land with a dull thud on the deck. With all her claws free, the Queen assumes attack position and prepares to strike.

Keeping your eyes on the Queen, you slowly shake your head. "I'm not locked up with you," you reply as you edge toward the guardrail. "You are locked up with *me*."

The Queen pounces. Choose to evade her, combat her using Power, combat her with a lightsaber, or fire the disruptor rifle at the Bartokk Queen.

To evade the Bartokk Queen: Roll the 20-dice to leap out of the way of the assassin. Your roll# + your stealth# + 2 is your adventure#.

If your adventure# is equal to or more than 14, add the difference + 15 to your AP total. You leap out of the way of the oncoming Bartokk Queen, and she slams headfirst into the durasteel bulkhead. The Queen is knocked unconscious, and you may proceed.

If your adventure# is less than 14, subtract the difference from your AP total. The Bartokk Queen anticipates your movement and prepares to attack again. Proceed to combat the Bartokk Queen using your weapon (below).

To combat the Bartokk Queen (using Power)": Choose your Redirect Power or (if you are a Jedi) your Force Movement Power. Roll the 20-dice to send the Queen flying backward. Your roll# + your Power# + your Power's high-resist# is your adventure#.

If your adventure# is equal to or more than 14, add the difference + 15 to your AP total. The Bartokk Queen's bulbous, multifaceted eyes widen with surprise as you send her flying into a wall. She collapses to the deck, and you may proceed.

If your adventure# is less than 14, subtract the difference from your AP total. You are unable to focus your Power on her. Proceed to combat the Bartokk Queen using your weapon (below).

*NOTE: This counts as one of three Power uses you are allowed on this adventure.

To combat the Bartokk Queen using your weapon: Choose your weapon. Roll the 20-dice to target the Bartokk Queen. If defense is one of your talents, your roll# + your weaponry# + your weapon's mid-range# + 2 is your adventure#. If defense is not one of your talents, your roll# + your weaponry# + your weapon's mid-range# is your adventure#.

If your adventure# is equal to or more than 15, add the difference + 15 to your AP total.

You may proceed. The battle is fierce, but ends with the Bartokk Queen lying motionless on the space yacht's deck. You may proceed.

If your adventure# is less than 15, subtract 8 AP from your AP total. The Queen is the deadliest Bartokk you've ever encountered, and she is as furious as she is fast. Roll the 20-dice again for your new roll#. If defense is one of your talents, your new roll# + your weaponry# + your weapon's mid-range# +3 is your new adventure#. If defense is not one of your talents, your new roll# + your weaponry# + your weapon's mid-range# +1 is your new adventure#.

If your new adventure# is equal to or more than 16, add the difference to your AP total. The Bartokk Queen is no match for your expert use of weaponry. The Queen is defeated, and you may proceed.

If your new adventure# is less than 16, subtract the difference from your AP total. Your weapon is out of energy! Proceed to fire the disruptor rifle at the Bartokk Queen (below).

To fire the disruptor rifle at the Bartokk Queen: The disruptor rifle has five settings, and you're unfamiliar with the weapon's alien design. But with the weapon in your grasp, you are determined to use it. Roll the 10-dice to blast the Queen with energy. Your roll# is your adventure#.

If your adventure# is 1 or 2: Subtract 5 AP from your AP total. You clicked on the disruptor's safety mechanism, which prevents the weapon from firing. You quickly release the safety. Roll again.

If your adventure# is 3 or 4: You fire at the Bartokk Queen, but she dodges aside and avoids the blast of energy. Subtract 7 AP from your AP total and roll again.

If your adventure# is 5 or 6: Add 15 AP to your AP total. You fire, and the disruptor releases a wide blast of high-energy particles at the Bartokk Queen. The Queen is defeated, and you may proceed.

If your adventure# is 7 or 8: The disruptor is out of ammo! Fortunately, your own weapon is now fully energized. Combat the Bartokk Queen using your own weapon (above).

If your adventure# is 9 or 10: Add 20 AP to your AP total. You fire the disruptor, striking a large fixture hanging over the Queen. It falls onto her, and she is defeated.

The SoroSuub space yacht veers off course, and the three surviving Bartokks step out of the main cabin. Teela Panjarra's conveyor begins to slide across the deck toward the cabin, but you grab hold of it. In less than twenty seconds, the plasma bomb will detonate. You must escape the SoroSuub space yacht before the three Bartokks can attack you or the bomb explodes.

There are only two ways off the enclosed stern. You can use the space yacht's emergency life pod or use your vehicle's weapons to blast through the canopy shields to allow you to escape. To escape from the space yacht, choose to use the emergency life pod or your own vehicle.

To use the emergency life pod: Roll the 10-dice to escape with Teela Panjarra in the yacht's escape pod. Your roll# + your skill# + your stealth# is your adventure#.

If your adventure# is equal to or more than 9, add the difference + 10 to your AP total. The escape pod blasts free from the space yacht, carrying you down to Curamelle city. You may proceed.

If your adventure# is less than 9, subtract the difference from your AP total. The three Bartokks block your path to the life pod. There isn't any time to fight the Bartokks! Proceed to use your own vehicle (below).

To use your own vehicle: Roll the 20-dice to fire your vehicle's laser cannons at the space yacht's canopy shield, then launch through the shattered shield and away from the yacht. Your roll# + your navigation# + your skill# + your vehicle's weaponry# is your adventure#.

If your adventure# is equal to or more than 17, add the difference + 10 to your AP total. Your laser cannons punch a large hole through the space yacht's canopy. You launch your vehicle through the hole, and you may proceed.

If your adventure# is less than 17, subtract 8 AP from your AP total. Your laser cannons blast through the yacht's canopy, but your repulsorlift engine stalls. You must start the engine and launch away from the yacht as fast as possible. Roll the 20-dice again for your new roll#. Your new roll# + your navigation# + your skill# + your vehicle's speed# is your new adventure#.

If your new adventure# is equal to or more than 17, add the difference + 5 to your AP total. With only seven seconds left on the plasma bomb's timer, your vehicle launches out through the ruined canopy shield and away from the space yacht. You may proceed.

If your new adventure# is less than 17, subtract the difference from your AP total. Your repulsorlift engine stalls again. Go back to "Roll the 20-dice again for your new roll#" and repeat. When you have launched away from the space yacht, you may proceed.

Zooming away from the SoroSuub space yacht, you place a protective hand over the viewport on Teela Panjarra's LOCC while you close your own eyes. Your escape craft is suddenly rocked by an incredible blast, followed by a thunderous boom. The plasma bomb detonated on schedule. Even with your eyes shut, you can see the intense light of the massive explosion.

The shock wave subsides, and your escape craft descends to the Science Service tower. You open the LOCC to check on

Teela Panjarra. She yawns, opens her eyes, looks at you . . .

. . . and giggles.

You have foiled the Bartokks' assignment on Corulag and rescued Teela Panjarra. Add 200 AP to your AP total.

To read the end of this adventure, turn to page 89 of your Star Wars Adventures novel, *Jedi Emergency*.